MASKS

JOHN VORNHOLT

Abridged and adapted by Joanne Suter

GLOBE FEARON
EDUCATIONAL PUBLISHER
PARAMUS, NEW JERSEY

Paramount Publishing

Printed in the United States of America
1 2 3 4 5 6 7 8 9 10 99 98 97 96 95 94

ISBN: 0-835-91106-3

GLOBE FEARON
EDUCATIONAL PUBLISHER
PARAMUS, NEW JERSEY

Paramount Publishing

CONTENTS

Characters v

Chapter 1 1

Chapter 2 12

Chapter 3 18

Chapter 4 27

Chapter 5 39

Chapter 6 50

Chapter 7 58

Chapter 8 66

Chapter 9 76

Chapter 10 88

Chapter 11 97

CHARACTERS

Crew of the *U.S.S. Enterprise*

Wesley Crusher—teenager, Acting Ensign

Data—Lieutenant Commander and android; serves as the *Enterprise*'s science officer and helmsman

Geordi La Forge—Chief Engineer

Jean-Luc Picard—Captain

Kate Pulaski—Doctor

William Riker—Commander and First Officer

Deanna Troi—Counselor

Worf—Klingon Security Chief

Other characters

Fenton Lewis—ambassador

Ferengi—space traders who place profits above everything else

Almighty Slayer—Lorcan head of state

Piercing Blade—Lorcan woman seeking the throne

The mask lay on the table. Its metal shone, even in the dim lights of the *Enterprise's* Ten-Forward lounge. Dark ribbons of black and blue covered the mask like a spider-web. Red, green and yellow jewels circled the eye-holes. A ring of black stones around the mouth added a stern look. The edges swept back in wings of purple feathers.

"It's beautiful," whispered Kate Pulaski. She reached for the mask. "May I hold it?"

A tall, strong-looking man stopped her hand. He was dressed in leather clothing and wore his sandy hair to his shoulders. "No, Doctor, you may not," Fenton Lewis said. "I don't want anything to happen to this mask before we reach Lorca. You see, it is my calling card."

Just then Ten-Forward's doors slid open. Jean-Luc Picard and William T. Riker entered. Though Riker was taller than Picard, there was no question who was in charge. The slim, balding Picard moved with strength and command. The crowd in the room parted to let the captain and his first officer pass.

"Ambassador Lewis?" Picard asked the unusual stranger. Then he spotted the mask. He leaned over it excitedly. "Is this mask really Lorcan?"

"A real Ambassador's Mask," said Lewis. "Feel free to look at it closely, Captain."

Riker smiled at his captain's unusual show of excitement. "This is Captain Jean-Luc Picard," he said. "I am Commander William T. Riker, first officer of the *Enterprise.*"

Captain Picard carefully lifted the Lorcan mask. "It's beautiful, but do you have any idea how rare these masks are? A Lorcan has to be killed to be separated from his mask. Isn't that true, Ambassador?" Picard noted.

"Not always," said the long-haired traveler. "Sometimes Lorcans have to fight to get their masks. But that fight is not always to the death. The Ambassador's Mask is one of the few that can leave the planet and be worn by off-worlders. I'm surprised you know so much about Lorca, Captain."

"I know little," Picard said. "But I am drawn by the place. It's like days of old. Imagine a place where the most dangerous weapon is a sword."

"Then perhaps you will come with me on my mission," Fenton Lewis said.

Commander Riker broke in. "Usually the first officer leads away teams. The captain is too important to risk."

"As the captain said," Lewis replied, "the Lorcans have nothing more dangerous than swords."

"Swords can kill," said Riker.

Captain Picard continued to look at the silver mask with its jewels and feathers. "How dangerous can a people be, who make something so beautiful?"

Picard handed the mask back to Fenton Lewis. "We'll reach the planet in eighteen hours. We will decide then who, if anyone, is to beam down to Lorca with Ambassador Lewis."

Some hours later Will Riker went to his room to sleep. He did not like Fenton Lewis asking the captain to join the away team. He hoped that Worf, as security officer, would agree that the captain should stay with his ship. There was something about Lewis that bothered Riker. He planned to watch the ambassador closely.

Riker sat at his desk. "Computer," he said. "Tell me about Ambassador Fenton Lewis."

"Ambassador Fenton Lewis," came the clear woman's voice of the computer. "Age: forty-six. Educated: Oxford University, Planet Earth. Offered a place at the Starfleet Academy. Turned it down to join a trading mission to the Klingon Empire. Was only survivor of a crash of the trade ship. Lived alone in the wilds of Orestes VII for three years. After his rescue, joined the Diplomatic Service. Twice won the Federation Medal of Honor. Wrote three books on wilderness survival. Present post: ambassador-at-large with special duties."

"Tell me," said Riker, "does the ambassador have any black spots on his record?"

"The Ferengi Nation has tried him for murder," answered the computer.

"Murder?" asked Riker, raising his eyebrows. "Just what happened between Lewis and the Ferengi?"

"That information has been pulled from the file," answered the computer.

Riker turned off the computer. He lowered the lights in his cabin to a warm yellow glow. He lay in his bed for some time before falling asleep.

The *Enterprise* was nearing Lorca. Riker stood on the bridge, rocking from one foot to the other. He looked like a teapot about to boil over. Why shouldn't he? Picard smiled to himself. Riker's job was to protect his captain from all dangers. But the captain had a mind of his own.

"Ensign Crusher," Picard said, "hold course at warp speed."

"Yes, Captain," Wesley Crusher answered.

"Number One, Worf, Data, La Forge, let's join Ambassador Lewis in the meeting room. I've asked Counselor Troi and Dr. Pulaski to meet us there."

The android, Data, and the Klingon, Worf, followed Picard and Riker off the bridge. Other crew members took their spots. When they reached the meeting room, they found Deanna Troi and Kate Pulaski looking at the mask. Lewis, it seemed, was not letting it out of his sight. The ambassador stood at the big windows watching the stars. His frontiersman's clothes made him look like someone out of a history book.

"What a sight," Lewis sighed. "With so much out there, it makes you want just a small piece of it for yourself."

"Ambassador," said Picard. "Let me introduce you. This is Lieutenant Commander Data. This is Lieutenant La Forge, our chief engineer, and Lieutenant Worf, our security chief.

Fenton Lewis's gaze met the android Data's steady yellow eyes. Then Geordi La Forge nodded to Lewis and smiled, his sightless eyes hidden behind his VISOR. The ambassador turned to Worf. He spoke in a strange language of growls and clicks. Worf looked surprised, then answered in the same tongue.

"I wish I had time to get to know each of you," Lewis said. "But we shall arrive at Lorca in a matter of hours. I have made a special study of the planet. I believe no one in the Federation knows as much about Lorcan ways as I do.

"Lorca was settled about two hundred years ago by two groups from Earth. One of them was a wandering theater company. In fact, the planet's name is taken from a famous Earth playwright. The group used Lorca as a place to practice new plays. The second group was a cult of anti-technologists. They were people who did not like the machinery of their age. They wanted a place to live a simple life. They hired the acting company to take them to Lorca in their ship. That was the last Earth ever heard of either group.

"Earth thought the ship was destroyed on the way to Lorca. It did, in fact, make it to the planet. Later on, sudden volcanic eruptions turned Lorca into a fire storm. Volcanoes shot out enough ash to lower the temperature by half. All technology was destroyed. Somehow, a thousand or so settlers lived through the eruptions. Over time, they have set up a warrior-run society. It is much like Earth during the Middle Ages."

Lewis held up the Ambassador's Mask. "The use of masks comes from the theater group. The whole society of Lorca is built around masks such as this one. Each Lorcan's standing is based on the type of mask he or she wears. A person of lower rank obeys a person of higher rank. A peasant wears a simple clay mask. A nobleman or noblewoman wears a metal mask with jewels. I don't mean they wear these masks at special times. They wear them *all* the time. Appearing in front of people without a mask would be just like walking naked through town."

Deanna Troi held up a hand to ask a question. Lewis nodded to the beautiful, dark-eyed crew member from the planet Betazed.

"Can these people move up from one social rank to another?" Deanna asked. "Can they just put on a different mask?"

"That," Lewis said, "is where fighting comes in. At any time, one Lorcan may challenge another's right to wear the mask of a certain rank. Sometimes they will duel. Most often these sword fights do not end in death. The winner will simply take a mask as a prize. If the mask is better than his or her own, he or she will wear it, thus rising in rank."

"Are these duels ever to the death?" Riker asked.

"Lorca is a violent planet," Fenton Lewis said. "But none of our information is certain. I am going there to get answers. Reports show that the planet may be in store for more volcanic eruptions. We will send a team of scientists, but first we need to open friendly relations. After all, we owe something to these people. They are of Earth stock, even if they hardly remember it."

Lewis frowned. "The Federation is also concerned because Lorcan masks have shown up at Ferengi art sales. You know the history of the Ferengi. We are worried that they might turn Lorca into one of their mining colonies. If Lorcans ask for protection, we'll be able to give it.

"On the other hand," he added, "maybe the Lorcans are too warlike to accept friends. One of the problems is that they don't seem to have a central government. Their head of state is called the Almighty Slayer. But, we are not sure that there really is such a person."

"Almighty Slayer?" asked Geordi.

"I hope he is real," said Fenton Lewis. "He is the one I'm going there to find."

So far, Captain Picard had listened. Now he spoke. "Ambassador Lewis, our orders are to take you to Lorca and to protect you. We must be sure you are safe. It will be my job to decide when the danger is too great and the mission should end."

"Then, Captain," said Lewis, "you must join me. How else can you tell if I am safe or not?"

Will Riker leaned forward. "As I said before, Ambassador Lewis, the captain stays with the ship. The first officer leads all away teams."

"I say that Captain Picard should come along,"

declared Lewis. "He can't decide if I am in danger unless he is there!"

"I will be there," Picard said slowly. "I know you do not agree, Number One, but I have decided. We will beam down with a small party. There will be myself, Ambassador Lewis, Security Chief Worf, and Counselor Troi. Since she can sense feelings and thoughts, Troi is best able to tell if the Lorcans are peaceful or dangerous."

Geordi broke the uneasy silence that followed Picard's words. "At least Worf won't need a mask," he joked. Even Riker smiled.

"All of you *will* need masks," said Lewis. "On Lorca your bare faces would be shocking."

Picard frowned. "All we have aboard are some Halloween masks. Would those do?"

"They would be perfect," said the ambassador. "They would never be challenged."

"Then, this meeting is ended." Picard rose.

Only Riker waited as the others left the room.

"You don't think I should join the away team, do you?" Picard asked his first officer.

"I don't trust Lewis," said Riker. "Did you know he was tried for murder?"

"By the Ferengi," said Picard. "They think that the Federation stands in the way of their trading. For all we know, you and I may be wanted for some crime by the Ferengi."

"All the same, Captain, I don't trust him."

"Starfleet gave him this job. If anyone can set up relations with Lorca, he can"

Three Halloween masks lay in the transporter room. There were boots and hooded coats for cold weather. Captain Picard saw the masks and smiled.

One mask was a grinning, white-faced clown. Another was the face of a pink pig wearing a tiny green top hat. The third was a red devil's face.

"They're the best I could find," said Troi.

"They'll be perfect," replied the ambassador.

"We'll carry hand phasers, set to stun," said Picard. "Remember the Federation's Prime Directive. We must not interfere with the ways of the planet. The people of Lorca are without technology. I don't want them to see the phasers or any other equipment that they might get curious about." He lifted one of the heavy coats. "Do we really need this gear?"

"It is freezing on Lorca," said Worf, "even though the volcanoes have made many hot springs."

Picard nodded. He pinned his communicator badge to one of the coats. Then he made sure his phaser was set to stun. "Data," Picard ordered, "don't set us down next to any life-forms. We don't want to frighten them."

The four team members pulled on the gear.

"To the grand adventure!" Lewis exclaimed. "To the Lewis and Picard Expedition!"

"Pardon me?" The captain blinked.

"One of my forefathers was Meriwether Lewis, of the famous Lewis and Clark expedition," said the ambassador proudly. "They were the first to map the American West. Exploring runs in my blood!"

"Let's hope our mission goes as well as Lewis and Clark's did," Picard replied. He walked to the transformer platform. Ambassador Lewis, Lieutenant Worf, and Counselor Troi followed. The captain nodded to Data.

"Energize," said Picard.

CHAPTER 2

The transformer set the away team down on a wide plain. Yellow-red mountains towered in the distance. They stood out against the dark red sky. The ground was orange but was dotted with puddles of blue-black water. Here and there spouts of steam shot into the air. They were blown to pieces by the wind. The *Enterprise* crew pulled their coats tight around them. Still, the cold crept in and bit their skin.

Jean-Luc spoke first. "Worf, have you seen any life-forms?" His words came out in frosty puffs.

"Over there, Captain," answered the Klingon. He pointed to a forest behind them. A wave of brown plants and trees began where the plain ended. A pack of red-furred creatures sat on the ground at the forest's edge. From time to time, one of the beings would reach up into the trees with its long arms. It would gracefully pull itself into the brown leaves. The creatures watched the strangers. They did not come closer, nor did they run away.

"I do not sense a high intelligence," said Deanna Troi.

"There will be time enough to study the animal-life later," said Lewis. "Let's find some people to talk to." He put on the Lorcan Ambassador's mask.

Captain Picard stepped forward. He gently tested the ground under his feet. It crackled where he stepped. It was hard on top, but the puddles were signs of underground hot springs made by volcanoes flowing near the surface.

"Meet some more Lorcan life forms," said Fenton Lewis. He picked up a handful of clay. Some of it was moving. "Worms," he said. "They are everywhere."

Lewis kicked at a stone. It rolled across the clay ground before plopping into one of the dark blue puddles. It quickly sank out of sight. "These are deep sinkholes," Lewis warned. "Stay away from them."

Everyone nodded. Deanna Troi managed a weak smile. She was beginning to wonder exactly what dangers Lorca held.

As if reading her mind, one of the far-off mountains suddenly blew up. It shot a fiery red cloud into the sky. The ground shook. The nearest sinkholes steamed and bubbled.

At once the Halloween masks became useful equipment. Picard, Worf, and Deanna pulled them out of their packs and tied them over their faces. A cloud of red ash and black sand swept over them.

"Head for those trees!" Picard ordered.

The party began to run toward the brown forest to the south.

When they reached the trees, the furry creatures were gone. They must have been frightened away when the volcano blew. Captain Picard continued to lead the way.

They marched through the brown forest. Only Fenton Lewis continued to wear his mask. Deanna looked at him. She had never known any other human whose mind control was so strong or so full of secrets. He was very careful to hide his true self, and the mask helped him.

"Trying to figure me out?" Lewis asked, surprising Deanna.

"The mask," she replied, "it suits you."

"What about you, Counselor? Are you missing that handsome first officer—Riker? Is that his name? You two were in love, weren't you?"

Deanna felt her face turn red, first with surprise, then with anger. "I had no idea that Federation ambassadors kept up on such things."

Fenton Lewis shrugged. "Just curious."

"Lieutenant Worf," Picard said to the Klingon. "You may contact the ship. See if they can warn us the next time a volcano's about to erupt."

"Yes, Captain." Worf tapped his communicator badge. There was no answering tone. He tapped it again. Then he looked at it closely. Black sand covered the badge. The sand was fine enough to work its way into the communicator.

Picard tapped his own communicator. He, too, was greeted with silence. "Troi, try yours."

Deanna touched it. It was dead.

Fenton Lewis began to laugh. "You know, I never liked the idea of pinning communicators on people's clothes. You should have kept them in your pockets." He laughed again.

"This is not funny," Captain Picard said.

"The crew will be worried," said Worf.

"Why?" asked Lewis. "They know where they set us down. All we have to do is go back to the original spot for beam-up. Isn't that right, Captain?"

"Yes. But Commander Riker will be upset. We should have checked in by now."

Suddenly the ground shook. The mountains again shot flaming clouds into the sky. No one needed to give the order to put on masks and take cover among the trees. Within seconds, Deanna Troi, Jean-Luc Picard, Worf, and Fenton Lewis had disappeared into the Lorcan forest. The red plain was bare.

"What do you mean, you've lost contact?" Riker asked Data.

"Just that, Commander. We have lost contact with the away team. In addition, the area where they beamed down is undergoing volcanic eruptions. Our sensors are not working. Even if the away team stayed on the beam-down spot, we could not lock onto them. We cannot beam them back up until the eruptions are over."

"I don't like it," Riker worried. "We must get our captain, Deanna, and Worf off that planet. Fenton Lewis can stay there forever if he likes!"

Will tapped his communicator. He had made a decision. "Riker to sickbay."

"Dr. Pulaski here," came the reply.

"Doctor, can you be ready to beam down to the planet in about twenty minutes?"

"Of course. Has something gone wrong?"

"We've lost contact with the away team. Meet me in the transporter room."

Riker tapped his communicator again. "Riker to Security. I want two officers in the transporter room in twenty minutes. This may be dangerous, so send me two people who can handle themselves."

"Request permission to join you, sir," said Geordi La Forge.

"I need you to stay home and mind the ship," answered Riker. "Don't send anyone else down to the planet. That is an order. If you don't hear from us in forty-eight hours, report to Starfleet."

"Yes, sir," Geordi replied. He looked at the big chair in the middle of the bridge. He was going to sit in that chair now. But he wasn't going to sit easily. He knew that.

"Commander?" asked Data. "May I join you in search of the captain and his party?"

"You may join us," agreed Will Riker.

Commander Riker strode into the transporter room. Dr. Kate Pulaski was already there. She was calmly checking over her medical supplies. The two security officers, Whiff and Greenblatt, stood at attention by the door.

Whiff was a giant humanoid with a smooth pink face. He was a new member of the Starfleet crew. Greenblatt was a small, blond woman. Riker remembered the tiny ensign from self-defense classes. He knew she could toss any one of them, including the huge Whiff, clear across the room.

The door to the transporter room slid open. Data came in. The party was ready. They pulled on their heavy coats, checked their phasers, and went to the platform. Pulaski suddenly looked worried, as if she had forgotten something important.

"Masks!" she gasped. "We don't have masks!"

"There's no time," snapped Riker. He checked to see that everyone was ready. "Energize."

CHAPTER 3

Riker's party materialized in a great forest. Huge brown trees stood on all sides of them.

Kate Pulaski looked up along the trunk of one of the towering trees. At the top, she saw clouds pink as cotton candy. She suddenly jumped back a step. A hairy creature was looking at her from the highest branches of the tree. It chattered loudly.

Whiff and Greenblatt pointed their phasers in its direction. The creature swung through the trees on long arms, always watching them.

"At ease," Riker told the security officers.

"It seems," said Kate Pulaski, "that it has seen humans before. It does not seem to be afraid of us."

"Which way should we go, Data?" Riker asked.

Data checked his tricoder. "I am picking up more life-forms to the west. One of the beings is quite large."

"Let's go," said the commander. They set off along a path between the trees.

Twigs snapped overhead. The same hairy

creature stayed right above them. It chattered happily.

"It appears to be following us," Data said.

Whiff had wandered ahead. Now he called back. "Commander Riker! I see a road!"

Seconds later the party discovered a dirt road. Wagon tracks and small hoof prints marked the red clay.

"Listen!" Ensign Greenblatt whispered.

From nearby came the sound of singing. It was a man's voice, and the sound was coming closer.

Riker motioned to the party to hide behind the trees.

A moment later, a brown pony came out of the woods. It was pulling a brightly painted wagon. Sitting in the driver's seat was what looked like a large sunflower. Riker knew that he was looking at a real live Lorcan, complete with mask. The mask was round and yellow with blue markings. The same markings were painted on the wagon. Even the pony was wearing a mask of blue.

Just then something streaked out of the woods. It landed on the roof of the wagon with a thud. It was the furry creature. It sat on the red wagon-top and gave an ear-splitting scream.

"Whoa!" shouted the driver, pulling back on his pony. "What is it, Reba?"

The thing jumped up and down. It pointed its long arms at the hidden off-worlders.

Commander Riker stepped out from behind a tree. "We mean you no harm!" he shouted.

"Demons!" cried the man in the mask. He hid his eyes. "Spare me! I am but a poor peddler!"

"We aren't demons," said Riker. He waved to the others to come out. "We are visitors."

"Demons!" the man yelled. "Make my death quick, I beg you." The animal, Reba, came down from the roof of the wagon. She hung onto her master's back. The two of them screamed together.

These were the fierce Lorcans? thought Riker. "Honestly," he said, "we mean you no harm. We are just visitors from a far-off place."

"Where are your masks?" the peddler demanded.

"We don't wear masks," Will answered.

"No *masks*? You should be put to death for such a thing!"

The Lorcan suddenly reached into the back of his wagon. He pulled out a large sword. Its handle was covered with jewels. "Pray for your souls!"

Whiff and Greenblatt stepped forward. Their hands were tight around their phasers. "Put that down!" Whiff ordered.

"Wait!" said Kate Pulaski. She stepped between Whiff and Greenblatt and spoke to the man in the sunflower mask. "If we agree to wear masks, will you help us? We are searching for our friends."

The sunflower lowered his sword a bit. "Will you be my servants? Will you follow and obey me?"

"Servants?" Riker spit the word.

"Only until after the fair," said the peddler. "With so many followers, I will be able to wear a Merchant's Mask and demand a large space to sell my goods."

"What kind of mask are you wearing now?" asked Data.

"A poor peddler's mask," said the Lorcan.

Data was interested. "What type of masks would we wear?"

"All right," sighed the peddler. "All of you may wear the Apprentice's Mask instead of the Servant's Mask. But you must obey me—at least in public."

The doctor moved closer to Riker. "I don't think we can go anywhere on Lorca without masks," she whispered.

"We'll wear the masks," said the commander. "But how long does this fair last? Our main concern is to find our friends."

"Surely they will be at the fair," said the peddler. "It is a fortnight away."

"That is two weeks," Data added.

"If we don't hit any boggles," said the peddler. He

tossed his sword back in the wagon.

"Boggles?" asked Pulaski.

"Fire storms," the Lorcan explained. "They can kill animals and people. The ground opens up. Fire flies in the air. You feel the hot breath of the dragon who lives at the center of the world."

"Volcanoes," said Data.

"The paint burns right off the wagon."

Riker pulled the Starfleet communicator off his jacket. "We'd better keep everything under cover. That includes the scanners and the phasers."

"Put your belongings in the wagon," said the Lorcan. He jumped to the ground. Riker was surprised how tall and fit he was. His voice had sounded very old. The masks hid a lot.

"I am Day Timer," he said. He took hold of Will's arm.

The commander grasped the Lorcan's arm. "Will Riker."

"Now, Will Riker, tell your servants to help me dig for clay."

"These aren't my servants," Will said. "They are my friends. Why should we dig for clay?"

"Because," said Day Timer, "you must have masks as soon as possible." His own mask turned toward Ensign Greenblatt. "I haven't seen the bare face of a woman in six years. You could put me to death for looking at her now."

Kate Pulaski stepped closer to Will. "Let's help him dig for clay."

Riker looked up at the darkening red sky. It had been a long day. They had gathered clay and picked out the worms. Then Day Timer had shaped five masks, all in perfect circles. He had built a large fire and set the masks nearby to dry. They would, he announced, be ready by morning.

Will pulled his communicator from the inside pocket of his jacket. "Riker to *Enterprise*."

"Hello, Commander Riker," came Geordi's eager voice. "How are you? Any luck yet?"

"As a matter of fact, no," grumbled Riker.

"We're keeping track of you all the time," Geordi said. "The transporter is ready to beam you back aboard round the clock. We're all with you. Let's get our captain and crew back."

"That's the plan," answered Will. "Thank you, Mr. La Forge. Riker out."

Riker turned to watch Day Timer. He was scraping the brown moss from tree branches before feeding them to the fire. The moss would not burn, he explained. That was how the giant trees could survive the volcanoes.

Suddenly there came a burst of chattering. Reba

dashed up. She carried six good-sized fish in her long arms.

"Reba has caught us our dinner," Day Timer explained. The bogs are full of fish, and the werjuns are excellent fishers. He scratched his pet's head. "Good werjun, Reba. Thank you."

The werjun chattered happily.

Day Timer cooked the fish over the fire. Kate Pulaski and Ensign Greenblatt sat away from the others during the meal. They did not want their bare faces to upset the Lorcan.

"Day Timer," Riker said, "before we came to Lorca, we heard of a great leader named Almighty Slayer. We think our friends have gone to find him. Do you know where we might find Almighty Slayer?"

"Almighty Slayer?" the Lorcan said. "I haven't heard that name in a long time. Yes, he was once a great warrior."

"Is he still your leader?" asked Riker.

"Yes," the peddler nodded. "If he still has the Wisdom Mask."

"The Wisdom Mask?" Data asked. "What is that?"

"The mask of the king. Whoever wears the Wisdom Mask rules all the land."

"Who decides who wears the mask?" asked Riker.

"The mask itself decides who its wearer shall be."

The small gathering was silent. The fire crackled.

Reba hung from the branches above them, fast asleep. The visitors stared at the fire, at the darkness all around them, and at the deep purple sky above them, filled with stars.

Riker, Whiff, and Day Timer spent the night near the fire. Ensign Greenblatt and Dr. Pulaski slept in the back of the peddler's little wagon.

In the morning the two women climbed out of the wagon. They came to the fire to get warm. Day Timer wandered off to avoid their naked faces.

"You wouldn't believe the junk he has in that wagon," Kate whispered to Riker. "He does, however, have two beautiful masks. One is of clay and feathers and another of wood and jewels."

Commander Riker lifted one of the masks that Day Timer had molded the night before. It was dry.

"Day Timer," he called to the peddler. The Lorcan came over and studied the new masks. He declared them ready for wear.

Commander Riker tried on his Apprentice's Mask. It fit perfectly. Day Timer took hold of the leather ties, one on each side and a third on the top. He tied them at the back of Riker's head.

The mask curled around Will's face. His steamy breath kept his face warm.

"How do I look?" he asked.

"Just like we do," answered Dr. Pulaski.

Indeed, the second away team, in their plain, round masks, looked like five dirty pennies.

The clay was smooth against Will Riker's face. He felt surprisingly comfortable in his new mask. He would be enjoying this strange visit to Lorca, if only he was sure the captain's away team was safe.

CHAPTER 4

The Lewis and Picard Expedition, as Fenton Lewis kept calling it, got an early start that morning. No one had slept well. Deanna had been bothered by a bad dream. In it, a space ship was blown up by a giant fireball.

Now they walked along a path through the brown forest. Ambassador Lewis led. He was followed by Captain Picard and Deanna. Worf brought up the rear. The Klingon checked the phaser in his pocket every now and then.

They came to a wider road. "Horses use this road," Lewis said. "Small horses. See the prints?"

Just a moment later, Worf's nose twitched. "Horses," the Klingon warned. "Someone comes. I smell them."

"Let's greet them openly," Picard said. "We need their help if we are to find this Almighty Slayer and get back to our ship."

Worf could smell the life-forms coming. Deanna Troi could sense them. They were intelligent, but full of anger. The feelings she sensed scared her.

Soon they heard the horses feet. "Phasers ready," Picard ordered. "Set to stun."

Flashes of color began to show between the brown trunks of the trees.

"I'm putting my mask on," Lewis said. "I suggest you do the same."

"Make it so," Picard ordered.

Deanna and Worf put on their Halloween masks just in time. In a moment the road filled with six colorfully dressed knights. They rode six tiny ponies that pranced to a stop.

The riders all wore masks. Each was a work of art as wonderful as Lewis's Ambassador's Mask.

At the front of the party, a tall woman warrior sat atop a strong-looking pony. Her mask was the largest of the lot. It was a five-pointed star made of the same silver metal as Lewis's. A lightning bolt of blue jewels shot across the mask.

The other masks were amazing, too. A wooden one pictured a snarling animal. Real fur and teeth formed the snout. Another was made of brown, white, and purple feathers. This feathered mask made its wearer look like an owl.

Two of the masks were very much alike. They were simple bronze circles. One of the bronze masks was worn by a man and the other by a woman. The sixth mask showed two snakes made of green jewels.

Deanna found herself guessing the warriors' ranks by their masks. The lightning bolt worn by the woman was the finest of them all. The only mask that even came close was Lewis's Ambassador's Mask. In fact, they might have been made by the same person. The green snake mask was the next finest.

The riders eyed the strangers' masks, too. Deanna wondered if all Lorcan meetings began by sizing up masks.

"Hello, Ambassador." The woman in the lightning mask spoke to Lewis. "I am Piercing Blade. I know your mask, but the masks of your servants are strange. I can't tell their rank."

"We are sorry," said Lewis smoothly. "We are strangers here. We do not know all the customs."

"I have seen your mask before," continued the lightning bolt. "It was made by the master, Fazool. It was given to the Ferengi ambassador two summers ago. You are not Ferengi, so I must question your right to wear it."

Picard remembered the murder charge that appeared on Lewis's record.

"The Ferengi did *sell* me the mask," Lewis said. "But I am an ambassador in full standing of the United Federation of Planets. I have a right to wear the Ambassador's Mask."

"I think not," said Piercing Blade. She drew a

short sword from the top of her boot. "I challenge your right to wear the Ambassador's Mask! I will have it from you—with or without your head in it!"

"We are peaceful visitors." The captain broke in. "We will gladly wear whichever masks you wish. We have come to this land only to speak with your leader, Almighty Slayer."

Now Piercing Blade leaned forward. "Do you know where he is? We have looked for him for one full cycle. He must be dead or in hiding. Either way, his claim to the Wisdom Mask is ended."

"We can work together to find him," Lewis said.

"Yes, we can," Piercing Blade replied. "If that is my wish." She grabbed a brown sack and threw it to the ambassador's feet. "Give us the Ambassador's Mask. Put this over your face."

Fenton Lewis tossed his long hair. "I will fight for my right to wear the Ambassador's Mask. Give me a sword."

"No!" snapped Picard. "Piercing Blade, we come here in peace."

Piercing Blade looked at the slim captain in his devil's mask. "We do not care about the rest of your masks. But the Ambassador's Mask is a great treasure. Spider-Wing, hand him your short sword."

The man in the feathered mask pulled a sword from his boot. He stuck it in the ground.

As soon as Lewis touched the sword, Piercing Blade jumped down from her horse.

"Lewis, give her the mask," said Picard. "It's not worth dying over."

"I don't plan to die, Captain."

The two masked fighters circled each other. It was hard to believe that one of them was from a space-going society from far away. Here, in the Lorcan woods, they were the same.

Picard, Worf, and Deanna, their faces hidden by the Halloween masks, stood frozen. Then Lewis jumped forward. Metal hit metal. The duel was on.

Picard drew his phaser. "Set to stun, Worf. Fire only to save the ambassador's life."

Fenton Lewis fought hard, but Piercing Blade was much better. Within seconds, he was falling back, trying to hold off her blows. Worf raised his phaser, but Picard stopped him.

Indeed, the woman warrior did not seem to want to kill Lewis, only to embarrass him. He finally tripped over a log and fell flat on his back. Piercing Blade put her sword against his neck.

"Enough!" barked Picard. "Spare his life!"

"I will," answered Piercing Blade. "I need all the servants I can get." She held out her hand to Lewis. "Give me the mask."

Fenton Lewis took off the mask. He handed it to her. "You'll pay for this," he growled.

Piercing Blade turned from his naked face. She grabbed the old sack and threw it at him. "Cover yourself!" Lewis pulled the bag over his head.

"Spider Wing," the leader cried, "you shall be our ambassador!" She gave the silver prize to the man in the feather mask. The Lorcans cheered.

"Thank you, my lady," Spider Wing said. He bowed. "I pray I am worthy of this."

"What about the others?" asked the woman in the bronze circle. "Their masks are strange."

"Whatever their rank," said Piercing Blade, "they will now serve me. They will join my party."

Jean-Luc knew they could end all talk with their phasers. But he remembered the Prime Directive. He would only use force in self-defense. However, he had to gain control quickly.

"We are not here to mix in your affairs," he explained. "We cannot become your servants or join your company, although we are honored to be asked."

"You refuse Piercing Blade?" asked the man in the bronze circle mask. "Do you not see by her Thunder Mask that she is a noblewoman?"

"We see," Picard replied. "But we came here as visitors. We don't plan to stay. We merely ask for safe passage in our search for Almighty Slayer."

"You *must* join my company," said Piercing Blade, "or I must join yours." Again, she drew her sword. Then she tossed a sword to the captain.

Picard surprised himself by catching it in mid-air. "Do I have any choice but to fight?"

"You can join our band."

"We would be happy to travel with you as friends, but not as servants."

"Then you leave me no choice," she said, rather sadly. She pointed her sword at Jean-Luc.

Jean-Luc whispered to Worf, "I hate to cheat. But if you see me point my sword up, stun her."

"With pleasure," Worf replied.

The battle was only seconds old, and Jean-Luc was already tired. Piercing Blade stopped the captain's best stroke with so much force that the sword almost flew from his hand. What a woman! he thought. Piercing Blade slashed at his legs, nearly cutting his knee. He grabbed the Lorcan's arm. He could feel smooth, firm muscle. But Piercing Blade was surprised by his sudden grasp. She tried to pull away. Picard raised his sword in the air.

The flash of light lasted less than a second. Piercing Blade fell like a puppet that had lost its strings. Her friends had no idea what had happened.

"We want no more trouble," shouted Picard.

"You have no more," said the man in the snake mask. The Lorcans got off their horses and bowed.

Piercing Blade sat up slowly. "I have been bested," she said, "for the first time in my life. The Thunder Mask is yours. We are your servants."

"Stand up," said Picard, giving her his hand. "I wish you would keep your mask. It suits you. We are not here to collect masks or servants or money. We're here to talk to your leader. Can you help us find the ruler, Almighty Slayer?"

"One who hides his mask is no king!" cried Piercing Blade. "If the Wisdom Mask is not at the fair, I will take the throne for the Thunder Mask!"

"Here, here," shouted the other Lorcans. "Lady Piercing Blade should rule!"

"Where is this fair?" asked Deanna Troi.

"In Cottage Meadow, about ten days ride from here," answered Spider Wing. "But you have no ponies." He thought a moment. "Perhaps you can trade us those unusual masks for some."

"Yes!" cried Cold Angel, nodding his animal's mask. He reached out toward Worf's pink pig mask.

When all was said and done, every member of the away team had a real Lorcan mask to wear. They found themselves with one pony, two Page's Masks, a feathered Messenger's Mask, and an ugly Trainer's Mask. No amount of talking, however, was able to get back the Ambassador's Mask. Spider Wing now wore it proudly.

Picard gave the two Page's Masks to Worf and Deanna. He kept the two higher-ranking masks for Fenton Lewis and himself.

But first he had to find Lewis. The embarrassed

ambassador had disappeared. Picard started along the road. Where was Fenton Lewis, he wondered. Just what was he up to?

"Lewis!" called Picard. "Ambassador Lewis!"

"Shut up, Picard. Quit your hollering," came the reply. Picard looked up and saw Fenton Lewis sitting high in a tree.

In a moment he had climbed down. His clothes were dirty with the brown moss, but he was smiling.

"Lucky you had the Klingon and his phaser at your side. What's the news about Almighty Slayer?"

"It seems whoever has the Wisdom Mask rules Lorca. But the mask has not been seen in some time. Piercing Blade and the others are headed to a fair. They plan to make Piercing Blade the new ruler."

"Sounds like quite a party," said Lewis. "I see you have new masks for us."

"Before we go anywhere together," Picard stopped him, "there are some things I need to know. Just how did you come by the Ambassador's Mask?"

Lewis sat on a log. He motioned to the captain to sit beside him.

"Once in a lifetime," he began, "a treasure like

the Ambassador's Mask comes along. It was at an illegal Ferengi art sale. I couldn't come up with enough cash, so I sold interests in the mask to two Ferengi traders. After the sale, they tried to kill me and take the mask themselves. I killed them in self-defense."

"Then you stole the mask," snapped Picard.

"I know Starfleet will find out. My career is over. This is my last mission. I never planned to return to Starfleet, but to stay right here. Now it looks like I may have your company."

Captain Picard shook his head. What should he do? To end the mission now would mean giving up a good chance at friendship with the Lorcans.

"Lewis," Picard said, "I'm not a jury. I can't decide if you are guilty of murder. We were sent here to set up relations with Lorca. You *will* help me complete that mission. If you don't, I'll have you thrown in prison at the next starbase. Now choose a mask. Let's return to camp."

Fenton Lewis looked at the feathered Messenger's Mask and the ugly Trainer's Mask. He chose the Messenger's Mask for himself.

"I'm ready to show my face again," he said as he pulled it on.

Picard tied the Trainer's Mask over his own face. Not only did it look like an animal, it smelled of warm fur.

Fenton Lewis laughed. "You have one thing going for you, Picard. Nobody will fight you for that mask. Nobody would want it!"

Picard and Lewis returned to the Lorcan camp. Worf and Deanna had joined Piercing Blade's band in setting up tents and building fires. In the masks, it was hard to tell which workers were Lorcan.

"Captain." Worf came to him. He pointed to the Lorcan now wearing the pig mask. "Cold Angel said that they passed a village yesterday. If I ride with him all night, we can be there by morning."

Cold Angel joined them. "I must go to the maskmaker's shop. This mask is lovely, but it's not fit for battle. I want it made stronger."

"We shouldn't split up," said Picard.

"Don't worry," said Cold Angel. He put an arm around Worf. "This lad will be okay with me."

Picard nodded. "Be careful, Worf. Get back to us sometime tomorrow."

The Klingon and the Lorcan climbed on two ponies. They rode off at a trot.

After a dinner of fish from a nearby bog, the camp settled down. The Lorcans went to their tents. Lewis, Picard, and Deanna Troi curled up by the fire. Before long the two men were snoring. But Deanna's mind would not rest. She sensed that someone was plotting against the others. She couldn't tell who it was. But the feeling was strong.

At last the Betazoid gave in to sleep. She knew she could not stop the mind from plotting. Its plan would become clear soon enough.

It did, indeed, become clear, and sooner than she thought it would. Deanna sat up, wide awake, just a short time later. By the firelight, she saw the figure of Captain Picard. He was curled up, asleep. But Fenton Lewis was gone.

CHAPTER 5

Deanna Troi gently shook Captain Picard awake. "Fenton Lewis is gone."

"Lewis?" Picard mumbled. He was still half-asleep. "Are you sure he's not somewhere nearby?"

The Betazoid shook her head. "I don't sense him anywhere in camp." Deanna looked into the night. No stars shone above the trees. Surely Lewis would not dash out into the darkness of Lorca alone.

"What is the matter with that fool?" asked Jean-Luc. "Deanna, do you think Lewis would desert us and try to stay on the planet himself?"

"Why not?" Deanna said. "What have we to offer him now that we're out of contact with the ship? He doesn't seem to think that Piercing Blade can help him get what he wants."

"What does he want?"

"At one time I would have said he wanted to serve the Federation. But now," Deanna shook her head, "so much is possible. If he found the Wisdom Mask, he could be king."

Picard turned his back on the night and watched the fire. "We have to be on the road with Piercing

Blade tomorrow so Worf can find us. We have no choice but to leave Ambassador Lewis behind."

Worf followed Cold Angel's pony as it raced through the dark woods. A branch whipped across his face. He was thankful for the Page's Mask he wore.

As morning turned the sky a misty gray, Worf and Cold Angel saw smoke through the trees ahead. They heard happy voices. The first villagers they met were children wearing brightly painted wood masks. They stared at Cold Angel in his pig mask.

"I knew this mask would get attention," Cold Angel whispered. "I will be the most famous animal trainer on Lorca."

But Worf was looking at the rows of red clay huts. They stood on stilts high above the ground.

Cold Angel pointed out other buildings. Each had a mask on its door. "There is a blacksmith shop. Here is a baker and, there, at the end of the street is the maskmaker. This town doesn't have an inn, but the maskmaker is a friend. He will feed us."

The maskmaker's shop was the largest in the village. The mask painted on the door looked like a human face. Strange, thought Worf, that the sign of the maskmaker would be the face he worked to hide.

A small fellow answered their knock. His mask was the face of a young man, but his wrinkled hands and bent body showed that he was old. He greeted Cold Angel, then reached out for his Halloween mask. "What is this made of? Do you have more?"

"Perhaps," said Worf. "But we would have to talk about trade with your leader. Do you know where to find Almighty Slayer?"

"Slayer?" said the maskmaker. "Why, he must be as old as I am. Is that what you came here for?"

"No, Trim Hands," said Cold Angel. "My new mask is lovely to look at, but not fit for battle. I would ask you to make it strong with metal or wood."

Trim Hands nodded. "I could do it. But you'll have to leave the mask for a fortnight. Come."

Cold Angel and Worf followed the old Lorcan into a workshop filled with masks. Trim Hands left his guests there. When he returned, he carried a green mask with puffed cheeks. "Take this Fisherman's Mask," he said to Cold Angel. "Wear it until you return for your mask."

Cold Angel turned away from them and replaced the pig mask with the Fisherman's Mask. He moved so quickly that Worf did not catch sight of his face.

"We are going to the fair at Cottage Meadow," Cold Angel told the maskmaker. "I'll pick up my mask on our way back."

"Trim Hands," Worf tried again, "are you sure you know nothing more about Almighty Slayer?"

"I know he wears the Wisdom Mask, the mask of a king. But I haven't seen it for many cycles." The maskmaker's voice became angry. "Perhaps if we had a real king, we could get rid of the raiders."

"We will have a *queen* soon," said Cold Angel. "I shall return from the fair with great news!"

"Great news would be no more raiders," growled the maskmaker. With that, he led his guests to a table set with two steaming bowls.

"Ah! Fish stew!" exclaimed Cold Angel.

Will Riker sat beside Day Timer in the peddler's wagon. Data, Dr. Pulaski, and the two security officers, Greenblatt and Whiff, walked behind them.

"These friends for whom you are searching— they must be very important," the peddler said.

Riker nodded his Apprentice's Mask. "They are good friends."

"I may be a nosy old man," said the Lorcan, "but is one of your missing friends a woman?"

The commander looked at Day Timer. He was glad that his feelings were hidden by a mask. The loss of Captain Picard would be horrible. But he could not even think about losing Deanna.

"We'll find them," he said, more to himself than to anyone else.

"If they have been to the village, we'll find out about it," the peddler promised. He pointed to the top of the trees. The sun was beginning to peek through. "That's smoke. We should be there in a few minutes. When we arrive, act like apprentices. Let me do the talking. Now, hold the reins," said the Day Timer. He ducked into the back of the wagon.

A moment later, the Lorcan came out wearing a different mask. This one was also made from clay, but it was much finer. Blood red feathers formed the eyebrows. Rich blue silk lined the edges.

"My Merchant's Mask," said the Lorcan proudly. "I had to trade two ponies for it. Today is the first time I've worn it."

Data had been looking around with worry. "Where is Reba?" he called to Day Timer.

"She hates villages," he explained. "Some townspeople eat werjuns. She'll find us later."

Soon the first stilt-huts came into sight. Riker and Day Timer climbed down from the wagon.

The party was greeted by children in bright

masks. "No phasers," Riker whispered to his crew. "Day Timer, we're putting our trust in you."

An adult came near. "I know that wagon!" she cried. "Aren't you Day Timer? I like your new mask!" Her own was plain cloth stretched over a wood frame.

"I'm a merchant now," bragged Day Timer. "These are my apprentices. If you will feed and water my pony, I will give you a new fire starter."

He turned to Riker. "Come to the maskmaker's hut. He will know if strangers have passed through."

"Doctor, would you come with us?" Will said to Kate Pulaski.

Day Timer loudly gave an order. "The rest of you, stay with the wagon until I return."

At the maskmaker's, the three travelers were greeted by the bent old man in the human-like mask.

"Old friend! It is I, Day Timer."

"Day Timer!" cried the maskmaker. "I see your fortunes have improved!"

"Indeed! I have five apprentices and am on my way to the great fair."

"Everyone is going to the fair," Trim Hands said. "To me, it's just another chance to meet up with raiders and robbers."

"Trim Hands, we are looking for friends of ours.

They are strangers and may not know our ways." Day Timer's voice lowered to a whisper. "They may not even be wearing masks. Have you seen any such travelers?"

The maskmaker shook his head. "The only ones through here were part of Piercing Blade's group. Just this morning two of them dropped off an unusual mask for repairs."

"An unusual mask?" asked Commander Riker.

"May I see it?" asked Day Timer.

"Why not? They said it was a Trainer's Mask, but it's not like any I've seen." The old man left the room. He returned with the Halloween pig mask.

Will and Kate hid their excitement. "Sir," said Will, "may I see that? Who did you say gave you that? Are you sure it wasn't a stranger?"

"It was one of the warriors who follows Piercing Blade. Cold Angel is his name."

Will turned to Day Timer. "Who is this Piercing Blade?"

The peddler's words were angry. "She calls herself a noblewoman. Really, she is little better than a raider. I hope your friends haven't met up with her!"

Suddenly frightened shouts and cries came from outside. The shouts turned to screams. Riker ran to the door. Day Timer grabbed a sword from Trim Hands's workbench and rushed after him.

The old maskmaker dropped to his knees. "Raiders! Raiders!" he cried.

By the time Kate Pulaski reached the door, villagers were running everywhere. Horsemen charged after them waving swords. Whiff had already knocked one of the red-masked horsemen off his pony and was wrestling with him. A sword cut into the security officer's arm, but that didn't stop him. He grabbed the raider by the hair. Red Mask fell to the ground.

Blood was everywhere. One villager stood to fight, and a raider stabbed him through the heart. Wounded townspeople crawled behind their huts. Raiders chased them down, killing the slowest ones.

A clay-masked figure reached up and rammed his sword under a raider's ribs. Kate Pulaski realized the man with the sword was Day Timer.

A raider with a long sword went after Riker. Will grabbed the man and pulled him off his pony.

They wrestled to the ground, but the raider broke away. Will grabbed his wrist. The two men fought for the raider's sword. Riker won it, but the Lorcan was on his feet again, reaching for his knife. Will pushed the sword into the man's chest, then stepped back, dazed. He watched the raider fall.

A red mask blurred in front of Kate's face. She saw a raised sword ready to stab her. Before the raider could strike, a blinding flash of light hit him. He froze. Then he fell to the ground.

The doctor turned to see Ensign Greenblatt standing by the wagon. The security officer gave her a thumbs-up sign. Then she aimed her phaser at another raider. This one, though, had seen enough. He turned his pony and galloped out of the village.

Meanwhile, Data was protecting a group of children. A raider came at the android with his sword. Data grabbed the point of the sword with his bare hand. No matter how much the raider pulled, the sword stayed steady, as if stuck in cement.

"I will not give it back," Data said.

The raider looked around. Seeing the others dead or gone, he let go of the sword and ran away.

The *Enterprise* team gathered at the peddler's wagon. Dr. Pulaski turned quickly to the injured Whiff. "I can stop the bleeding," she said, "but we really should send him to sickbay. Data, take Ensign Whiff into the wagon. Use your communicator to have him beamed up to sickbay."

Kate saw Riker looking at the raider he had killed. "I saw it," she said. "You had no choice."

"That doesn't make me feel better," Will said.

For the rest of the day, Kate patched up the wounded Lorcans. She could do a better job if she took them back to the *Enterprise*, but the Prime Directive would not allow that. It did allow crew members to protect their own lives in an attack.

"Doctor, are you finished?" Riker called to Kate as she smoothed down the last bandage. "Day Timer says the villagers want to thank us for our help. This may be our chance to get going."

The villagers had gathered around Day Timer's wagon. Trim Hands coughed and began. "Today is a great day. Our village turned away a raider attack. We would like to show our thanks with masks."

Day Timer nodded, and Trim Hands went on. "To the one called Doctor, we present the mask of the Healer." He held up a yellow mask with two green snakes in its center. He handed it to Kate Pulaski. Its paint was still wet.

"You do not need to wear the mask now," Day Timer explained. "This morning it was a red mask worn by a raider. Now it is a Healer's Mask."

"Thank you," she said. "I am very pleased."

Trim Hands nodded. "Now, we honor the one called Data who protected our children. We present him with the Teacher's Mask." He took up a white mask covered with strange writing and signs. It was the first smiling mask the newcomers had seen.

"I will treasure it always," Data said.

"To the one called Greenblatt, who felled a raider with a fire arrow, we present the Archer's Mask." Trim Hands brought forth a black mask with blue and white arrows streaking across it.

Now the maskmaker grew quieter. When he spoke, his voice was sad. "This next mask is to honor the one called Whiff, who is no longer with us." Riker had explained Whiff's disappearance by saying he was dead. He said that Data had buried the body. "This mask is still red," continued Trim Hands. "We give it to you to remind you of your brave friend."

The crowd cheered. Then Day Timer stepped forward. He held up his hand. "The maskmaker has allowed me to present this next mask. Brave Will Riker has earned this special honor."

Day Timer went to his wagon. He returned with a mask called the Forest Mask. Its shiny wood looked like a glowing tree. Jewels made tiny leaves.

Will's hands were shaking as he took the mask. "I don't know what to say. This is an honor."

Now the Lorcans roared their cheers. Kate Pulaski was caught up in a happy crush of villagers. In the sea of colorful masks, she forgot for a moment about the missing away team. She forgot the *Enterprise* and the reason they came to Lorca.

For that moment, she was a Lorcan.

CHAPTER 6

Captain Picard looked back over his shoulder. Where were Worf and Cold Angel? They should have caught up by now.

Perhaps they ran across Fenton Lewis. The captain still couldn't believe that a Federation ambassador had deserted them.

"Picard," said a husky voice beside him, "I cannot see your face, but I feel you are troubled."

Jean-Luc turned to see Piercing Blade walking beside him. "I'm worried about Worf and Cold Angel," he said.

"You worry too much, Picard. Both men are loyal. They will join us as soon as they can. We will make camp and give them a chance to catch up. I know a bog where the fishing is good."

The Thunder Mask turned from him, and he caught sight of Piercing Blade's copper-colored hair. It curled around the back of her neck. For such a strong woman, she had a surprisingly slim neck.

Jean-Luc blushed under his mask. Here he was, a

starship captain, staring at the woman like a lovesick teenager.

When Piercing Blade turned back to him, her green eyes sparkled from behind the mask. "I would like you and your female page to dine with me. Come to my tent tonight," she said.

He nodded. He was glad that his feelings were hidden by a mask. "It will be our pleasure."

"Good. Now, I must look for that bog if we are to have anything to eat."

The warrior walked to the front of the party. Her long legs carried her quickly. The captain decided not to follow her. He would see her at dinner that night. He found he could hardly wait.

Cold Angel and Worf stopped near a bog to water their ponies. Fresh prints in the road showed they weren't far behind Piercing Blade's band.

Worf patted his pony's neck. "These are fine little animals," he said.

Cold Angel nodded. "I raised them myself."

"Do you have a farm somewhere?" Worf asked.

"Lady Piercing Blade has a wonderful home, far to the west," Cold Angel said proudly. "We've seen too little of it in the last months."

"Then you have been a long time searching for Almighty Slayer?"

"A long time," growled the Lorcan, "trying to get people to accept Piercing Blade as queen. Change is hard on Lorca. People like the old ways and the old stories. Slayer was a great warrior who settled many fights, but his time is past."

"How important is it for the ruler to have the Wisdom Mask?"

"I can't believe how little you strangers know. A ruler who didn't wear the Wisdom Mask might be accepted by some, but not by all. Many Lorcans believe the Wisdom Mask *chooses* the ruler of Lorca. That kind of thinking is hard to overcome."

Piercing Blade's band made camp. Fish were caught and cooked over the fire. Picard and Deanna Troi went to Piercing Blade's tent.

As soon as they arrived, the tent flap swung back. Piercing Blade met them in a long gown of white feathers. Jean-Luc felt as if he were looking at an angel.

"Please come in," she said. "I'm sorry I have nothing better than saddles to offer as chairs."

The two Lorcan pages entered with plates of steaming fish. Piercing Blade sat on the floor with her plate on her lap. "Eat," she commanded.

"I have one question for you tonight," she said. "Will you support me at the fair?"

"We cannot take sides in your planet's affairs," said Picard.

"Why not?" asked Piercing Blade. "Do you support someone else?"

Deanna spoke. "We come from far away in space. We cannot meddle in your lives. But we would like to be friends. You are not alone among the stars."

"Yes, the stars," said Piercing Blade. "You and the Ferengi remind us that the first Lorcans came from the stars."

"What do you know about your past?" asked Jean-Luc.

"The storytellers say our ancestors flew in a huge airship. But after they came here, the dragon who lives at the center of the world breathed fire. Flames rose and swallowed the whole ship."

Deanna leaned forward. "That would explain my dream. Captain, I believe the theater group's spaceship was just above the planet when a huge volcano blew. It destroyed the ship. It also put a cloud around the planet that made the weather colder. Ever since then, these people have been left to themselves. All their technology was destroyed in the eruption."

"Their masks are part of their theatrical past," said Picard.

"You two would make good storytellers," said Piercing Blade. "But the past is past. Why are you here now? The Ferengi come to trade. They want the fire-proof moss from our trees. What do you want?"

"We want your friendship. That is all," said Jean-Luc. He leaned closer to Piercing Blade.

Deanna suddenly felt that she was no longer needed. "Well," she said, "that was a fine dinner. Now I must be going."

Neither Picard nor Piercing Blade stopped her.

"I will watch for Lieutenant Worf or Ambassador Lewis," Deanna said.

A moment later, Picard and Piercing Blade were alone. The lamplight flickered. The tent was quiet and warm.

Piercing Blade put her plate aside. She stood up, tall and slim. "I have something to show you, Picard."

"What is it?"

"My face."

Picard rose to stand facing her.

"This is not easy for me," she whispered.

"Let me show you myself first, then," said Picard. He took off the Trainer's Mask. He smiled.

Piercing Blade's eyes widened in the eye-holes of her mask. She stepped closer to Picard. She touched his slim nose and his cheek.

Then she reached up to the strings of her own mask. It fell away from her face.

Picard gasped. He was not prepared for such a pale and beautiful face. He touched her cheek. Having never been bare to the sun, Piercing Blade's skin looked years younger than she was.

But the face was not perfect. A scar ran from her hairline to her nose. Jean-Luc ran his finger along the scar. Then he kissed her.

But the quiet of the tent was broken. Voices were calling. Piercing Blade moved away. She picked up her mask and motioned to Picard to do the same. "What is it?" she called.

"Cold Angel and the new page have returned," called Spider Wing. "The new page felt the trainer should be told."

Piercing Blade smiled at Picard. She pulled the Thunder Mask over her head. "You must go."

He sighed. "I have been honored tonight," he said before pulling on the Trainer's Mask.

"As have I," she replied. "I am so glad you are with us."

Jean-Luc left the tent. There was nothing more to say that night.

Day Timer and his party had a long way to go to get to the fair. The old peddler decided they should leave the village that night.

They moved carefully among the dark trees. Will

Riker reached up and rubbed the polished wood of his Forest Mask. He felt he had been accepted by the Lorcans. So had the others.

"Whoa!" Day Timer called softly to his pony. "Riker," he whispered, "there is someone up ahead."

The entire party froze. "Maybe it's Reba," said Will.

"Reba would jump right on the wagon and give me a hug," replied Day Timer.

Ensign Greenblatt drew her phaser.

"We mean no harm," called Riker loudly.

"The road is wide enough for all to pass," said Day Timer.

In the shadows just ahead stood a figure. It waited for a moment. Then it walked toward them.

"I mean you no harm either," said a man's voice. "I am alone."

Will could finally see the mask. It was covered with white, brown, and purple feathers.

"Good evening, Sir Messenger," called Day Timer. "You must have an important message. But you've no need to hide from us."

"Forgive me," said the man. As he bowed, his hair tumbled over his shoulders. "I was afraid because I didn't know who you were."

"Wait," said Data. "I know that voice. You are Ambassador Fenton Lewis, are you not?"

The man stepped back, shocked. He stared at the masks. Then he began to laugh. "This is rare!" he howled. "Is that the android?"

"Ambassador?" Riker tore off his mask.

"Riker!" Lewis exclaimed. "I never thought I would be glad to see *you*!"

"Where is the captain?" asked Kate Pulaski. "Where are the others?"

"You've heard nothing?" asked the ambassador. He took off his mask. "I must give you bad news."

"What is it?" asked Riker.

"Captain Picard and the others are dead."

"What?" gasped Kate Pulaski. "The captain is dead?"

"We were attacked," Lewis said, "by a band of thieves. They were led by a woman."

"Piercing Blade!" exclaimed Day Timer.

"We didn't have time to get her name," Lewis said.

"You're the only one left alive?" asked Riker. There was doubt in his voice. "How did that happen? How did you come by that mask?"

"After the volcano erupted, our communicators were dead." Lewis pointed to the trees. "We went into the woods, looking for cover. But there are more dangers here besides volcanoes. We were attacked. The ambassador's mask saved my life. The others were killed. I was taken prisoner. The Lorcans took my mask. They gave me this one to cover my face." He pointed to the feathered mask.

"Not possible," growled Day Timer. "Piercing Blade is tricky, but she isn't one to attack from hiding. She might kill one or two in a duel, but—"

"One or two!" snapped Fenton Lewis. "She's a

murderer, I tell you." He turned to Riker. "I have been through a great deal, Commander. I don't like having my word questioned."

Riker didn't like or trust this man. But he couldn't forget the Halloween mask in the maskmaker's shop. He had seen the violence on Lorca firsthand.

"Can you show me the place where this happened? I can't report anyone dead until I find the bodies."

"Very well," said Lewis. "I'll do my best to find the spot, but I'm not promising anything."

The party moved on with Lewis in the lead. Even Day Timer was quiet. He could feel his new friends' sorrow.

Kate and Riker walked side by side. "Are you going to call the *Enterprise* and let Geordi know?" Kate asked.

"I don't want to," said Will, "until we find them. As far as I'm concerned, they're still missing."

"You think he could be lying?" whispered Kate.

"Don't you?" asked Riker.

Following behind Riker and Pulaski, Data was going over all the information. He did not accept Fenton Lewis's story. Why would cold-blooded killers spare one life out of four? His biggest doubt came from the ambassador's new mask. It was a very fine one. Why would they give their victim a valuable mask? Indeed, Fenton Lewis was alive and well. That fact suggested to Data that the whole party was still alive.

Geordi La Forge sat in the captain's chair. He stared at the viewscreen and at the orange clouds of Lorca moving below the *Enterprise*.

"Mr. Crusher," he said. "How long has it been since we heard from Commander Riker?"

"About fourteen hours, sir," answered the teenager.

"When we last talked to him, his party was having dinner in a village. Now it's morning on Lorca."

"See if you can raise them."

"*Enterprise* to Commander Riker," called Wesley.

"Riker here," came a tired voice.

"This is Geordi, sir. We haven't heard from you in fourteen hours. Any news? Any word about the captain?"

There was a pause. "Nothing official," Riker finally said. "Geordi, I'd like to talk to you alone."

La Forge went to the captain's ready room. The door shut behind him. "What is it, Commander?" he said.

"We found Ambassador Lewis. He is alive and well," sighed Riker.

"That's great!" exclaimed Geordi.

"No," answered Will. "Lewis says that every other member of the first away team was killed by bandits. He says they're all dead—the captain, Worf, Deanna."

Geordi sat down heavily. "I can't believe it."

"But we haven't seen any bodies," Riker went on. "Certain parts of Lewis's story don't make sense. These death reports are *not official*. The first away team is still missing. We are still looking for them. That's all you are to tell anyone. Is that understood?"

"Understood. La Forge out."

"Ensign Crusher to Lieutenant La Forge. Urgent!"

"Lieutenant La Forge here. What is it, Wesley?"

"Sir," gulped the teenager, "we're not the only ones interested in Lorca. A Ferengi ship has just warped into the area. It is right above the planet."

"Have you tried to hail the ship?"

"No, sir. I was waiting for you."

In less than a second the bridge door whooshed open. Lieutenant La Forge rushed in. "What are the Ferengi doing?" he asked.

"Just sitting there," answered Wesley. "No shields, no weapons being armed."

"We're not at war with the Ferengi," said Geordi. "We have no reason not to be friendly."

"Scanners show that the Ferengi vessel has just

beamed a team down to the planet," reported Wesley.

"Hail their ship," ordered Geordi.

Wesley tried to call the Ferengi, but their ship would not reply. "Looks like they don't want to talk," he said. "The Ferengi don't care about anything but making money. If we can't help them, they don't want to deal with us."

"Let's look at the bright side of this," said Geordi, sinking into the captain's chair. "The more eyes and ears on that planet, the better. If we don't run across the captain, maybe the Ferengi will."

Commander Riker stared down the red road. "Blast the stars, Lewis! Don't you have any idea where this attack took place?"

Lewis kicked a lump of wormy clay. "I'm sorry, Commander. One stretch of forest looks like another."

Riker's communicator beeped from within his pocket. He pulled it out. "Riker here," he answered.

"This is Lieutenant La Forge. Commander, a Ferengi ship is sitting above the planet."

"Ferengi!" exclaimed Will. "What do they want?"

"I hailed them," said Geordi, "but they won't answer. They have already beamed a team down to Lorca."

"Keep them under close watch," said Riker. "Out." Then he turned to Fenton Lewis. "Which direction shall we go, Ambassador? It's up to you. We're not leaving this planet until we find those bodies."

Jean-Luc Picard looked down on the forest floor from the branches of a tree. He and Worf had separated from the Lorcans to search for the missing ambassador. But Worf had spotted red masks moving through the woods. They had learned that the red masks meant bandits. They had decided to hide and avoid a meeting, at least until they could size up the situation.

A twig cracked. From the brush, at least five red-masked Lorcans appeared. They were on foot. Their swords were drawn and ready. Soon another four Lorcans with red masks appeared riding ponies. The troop was followed by two more riders, but these two looked different. They wore silver masks, wide enough to cover huge ears.

Worf mouthed the word "Ferengi."

Jean-Luc nodded. Why, he wondered, were two Ferengi traveling with Lorcan outlaws?

Picard and Worf waited until the band passed. Then they climbed down from the tree. Picard drew his phaser from his pocket. "Set to stun," he said.

The captain and the Klingon strode through the woods until they saw the raiders and the Ferengi ahead. The sound of their footsteps brought the party to a halt.

"Peace," said Picard. His phaser was hidden in his hand. "We wish only to talk and share the road."

The wall of red masks stared at them, surprised. Few Lorcans dared to walk right up to a band of raiders. At last one of the raiders spoke. "You are brave, Trainer. So, we will let you speak before we kill you."

"Is this the way Ferengi greet fellow traders?" asked Picard.

"Who are you?" demanded one of the Ferengi.

"On Lorca, I am an animal trainer." Jean-Luc touched his mask. Then he pointed to the sky. "But up there I am Captain Jean-Luc Picard of the *Enterprise*."

The silver mask nodded. "We saw your ship."

"We have lost contact with the *Enterprise*. To put it simply, we need your help to get back."

"Ah," said one of the Ferengi. Picard could imagine the grin behind his mask. "Then you want something from us. What do you offer in return?"

"These masks," said Jean-Luc, "and our thanks."

"Not enough," said the Ferengi. "Your masks are very ordinary, and your thanks are worth nothing."

"What do you want?" asked Picard.

The Ferengi leaned forward. "The Wisdom Mask."

"If we knew where it was, we wouldn't need you. The whole planet would be at our feet," said Picard. "What about the Ambassador's Mask?"

"You stole that mask from us!" cried the Ferengi.

"Not I," said Picard. "Ambassador Fenton Lewis stole it at an auction. We are sorry for that, but he wasn't acting on the part of the Federation."

"Picard, we will get you to your ship in return for either the Wisdom Mask, or the Ambassador's Mask *and* Fenton Lewis."

"I might be able to get you the Ambassador's Mask," answered Picard. "But we don't know where to find Lewis. Will you at least call the *Enterprise* for us?"

"You've heard our offer," said the Ferengi. "Now be on your way."

The rest of the raiders backed up. They stood aside as Worf and Picard moved past and headed down the road.

"Remember our price," a Ferengi called after them. "It's the Wisdom Mask alone, or the Ambassador's Mask *and* Fenton Lewis."

CHAPTER 8

Just before they broke camp the next morning, Day Timer gathered his band. It was now made up of a nobleman, a healer, a teacher, an archer, and a messenger. Day Timer, himself, had gone back to wearing the simple Peddler's Mask.

"Starting today," Day Timer told them, "our trip becomes dangerous."

Kate Pulaski frowned behind her Healer's Mask. She wondered how anything could be more dangerous than what they had already faced.

"From this point, we will meet more travelers," Day Timer explained. "Not all will be friendly. With your new masks, you have become people of importance. Especially you, Riker. Everyone will want to talk to the wearer of the Forest Mask."

Day Timer climbed aboard his blue wagon and snapped the reins. The others marched behind.

"Whoa!" Day Timer suddenly stopped his wagon. Greenblatt hurried to the front to see what was happening. She returned a moment later.

"There is a crossroad up ahead. We can see at

least two riders down there. Day Timer wants the commander to get in the wagon."

"I'm not going to hide," said Riker.

"Part of Day Timer's plan," explained Greenblatt, "is to keep our strength hidden. He says we must be able to surprise our enemies."

"All right," Riker agreed. "Doctor, you and I will hide in the wagon. Data, if they look friendly, ask them about the captain. Greenblatt, keep an eye on Ambassador Lewis."

The doctor and the commander got in the back of the wagon and shut the door. The pony moved on. Data and Ensign Greenblatt followed behind. Greenblatt reached for her phaser. She remembered too late that it was inside the wagon.

Data looked around for Fenton Lewis. But the Ambassador had managed to drift off into the forest where he could stay out of sight.

Two riders sat at the crossroad on ponies. Their masks were plain silver metal. Sweeping wings almost hid their huge ears. These travelers were Ferengi. Data did not find this surprising since a Ferengi ship was above the planet.

"Good morning to you," Day Timer called to the Ferengi. "Will you allow my simple wagon to pass?"

"Where are you headed?" asked one Ferengi.

"To the fair at Cottage Meadow," the peddler answered. "Go on," he barked to his pony.

The big-eared trader rode out in front of the wagon. He forced the peddler to stop. The Ferengi pulled a whip from his saddle. "You're a peddler, aren't you? We want to see what you have to sell."

"I have nothing for fine noblemen like you," said Day Timer.

The other Ferengi moved closer. "Do you have masks for sale?"

"Only clay ones, fit for peasants."

"We'd like to look."

"Then come to the fair," said Day Timer in a friendly tone. "I'll have my own place there."

"We'd like to look at you wares now. I don't understand why you don't want to show them. We pay well, especially for fine masks."

The Ferengi pointed to Ensign Greenblatt in her handsome Archer's Mask. "What about you? How much will you take for that mask you are wearing?"

"It's not for sale," answered Greenblatt.

Data felt it was time for him to speak up. "You are Ferengi," he said. He spoke loudly enough for those inside the wagon to hear. "We are Lorcans. We have more right than you to travel this road. Why do you bother us?"

"Please let us pass," added Day Timer.

"I think not," the nearest Ferengi said. He snapped his fingers. At once, the trees shook. Red-masked Lorcans sprang out of the forest waving swords. They growled like wild animals.

Data moved toward the wagon. "Surrounded by raiders," he said loudly. "A large party."

"Who are you talking to?" a Ferengi asked. "How did you know I was a Ferengi?"

Inside the wagon, Riker held the communicator close to his mouth. He whispered, "Riker to *Enterprise*. Keep your voice down when you answer."

"Understood," Wesley Crusher whispered back.

"Wesley, I have no time to explain. We've got trouble. I need something to get the attention off of us. Can you cause a mild earthquake down here?"

"Uh, sure." The teenager sounded puzzled. "A small torpedo would do it. Just a little explosion would set off some shaking."

"Try it," said Will. "In sixty seconds. Out"

The commander handed a phaser to Kate. "I know you hate these things, Doctor, but use it if you have to."

"Who's inside there?" demanded an angry Ferengi voice. "I hear voices in the wagon!"

Will kicked open the door. He jumped out. Kate stayed hidden inside.

"The Forest Mask!" exclaimed one raider.

Riker strode to the center of the crossroad. Many of the red-masked Lorcans lowered their swords.

"He is a follower of Almighty Slayer," said one raider. "He may know where the Wisdom Mask is."

"How much will you take for that mask?" exclaimed one Ferengi. "Do you have more like it?"

Riker did not answer. He looked at the raiders. "Fellow Lorcans," he said, "the dragon who lives at the center of the world is unhappy. He cannot understand why you turn against your own people to help these strangers."

"Shut up!" growled the Ferengi. "Or I will silence you!"

Where are you Wesley? thought Riker. Come on, *Wesley*!

Wesley Crusher stood before the weapons panel on the bridge of the *Enterprise*.

"Torpedo away," he announced. He pressed a flashing red button.

The missile hit a mountain peak. The mountain exploded. Hot rock flew into the air. This blast set off another. A ring of volcanoes spit fire.

The forest shook wildly. Trees swayed. Branches crashed to the ground. Somehow, Riker stayed on his feet. The Ferengi in front of him wasn't so lucky. His pony dumped him and ran.

The Ferengi stood up and started to come after Riker with his whip. But he was knocked off his feet by one of the raiders. The red-masked Lorcan rushed past him screaming in fear.

The sky turned blood red. It became as dark as night. Riker stumbled, calling his friends' names. Finally he felt someone grab his arm. He was disappointed to find it was Fenton Lewis.

"Beam us out of here," Lewis yelled.

"Are you kidding?" Riker barked. "They couldn't even find us in this."

Lewis grabbed Riker by the collar. "You've got to try. We've got to get out!"

Will pushed him away. "Doctor! Greenblatt! Data!" he called.

Suddenly something clubbed him on the back of his head. Riker fell to the ground.

When the ground started shaking, Deanna Troi grabbed Captain Picard's arm. Worf stood beside him, ready to protect his captain. Until the darkness came, Captain Picard managed to keep an eye on the whole party. He could see Cold Angel trying to comfort the ponies. He could see Piercing Blade gathering her band together.

Then came the red darkness. Jean-Luc could still feel Deanna and Worf beside him. He wanted to run to Piercing Blade's side, but he knew he belonged with his own crew. He tried to keep on his feet. He hoped the planet would stay in one piece.

Lieutenant Geordi La Forge burst onto the bridge. He waved his arms. "What is going on down there?" he barked.

"I was just obeying orders," said Wes.

"Keep trying to reach Commander Riker," Geordi ordered. "Ensign Crusher, I want a full report."

"I've reached Lieutenant Commander Data," said Wesley. "But the signal is weak."

"Data, this is Geordi. How is everybody?"

"Unknown at present," answered Data. He was rising from his knees beside Will Riker. Day Timer was carefully removing Riker's Forest Mask. Fenton Lewis walked back and forth.

Data continued. "I am fine. Commander Riker is with me, but he has been knocked out. Ambassador Lewis is present, but I cannot find Dr. Pulaski or Ensign Greenblatt."

"I can't tell you how sorry we are about what happened," said Geordi. He glared at Wesley. "Obviously something went wrong."

"Ensign Crusher couldn't have done anything else," said Data. "I heard the commander's orders. We were about to be attacked by Ferengi and

Lorcan raiders. The explosion was larger than we would have wished, but it did rid us of our attackers."

"I see," answered Geordi. He nodded at Wesley.

"I think I see Dr. Pulaski," Data said. "I will contact you again later. Out."

Kate Pulaski limped down the road, leaning on Ensign Greenblatt. "Just my ankle," she called to Data. As soon as she saw Riker lying on the ground, she made her way to his side.

Ensign Greenblatt was carrying a strange mask. Day Timer quickly grabbed it from her.

"I'm sorry, Day Timer," said Greenblatt, "but the shaking scared your pony. She ran head first into a tree. She's dead, and there is not much left of your wagon. I found that strange mask, though."

Day Timer hid the mask close against himself. "It's nothing, just an old mask." He moved away.

"He's acting pretty strange," said Fenton Lewis. "Did anyone get a good look at that mask?"

A moan came from the ground behind them. They turned to see Commander Riker trying to sit up.

"Just a moment," Kate said. "You've had quite a knock on the head."

Riker blinked his eyes. He was happy to see his

friends. Then he saw the Messenger's Mask, and he exploded. "You hit me!" Riker yelled at Fenton Lewis. "You're the one who knocked me out!"

"You're crazy," said Lewis. "A branch hit you."

"The Ferengi and the raiders have run off," reported Data.

Riker rubbed his head. "If the Ferengi are helping the raiders, it means they want something. I'm afraid the Ferengi will try to make slaves of the whole population. They've done it before on other planets."

"The Lorcans need the Federation to help them," said Kate. "How can we make them see that?"

Riker shook his head. He was angry with himself. He had nearly been killed. The captain might be dead. They were risking too much on Lorca. "We can't just stumble around here, getting nothing done," he said. "The *Enterprise* needs us."

"We need you, too," came a voice.

They turned to see a familiar figure in an unfamiliar mask. Gone was the simple peddler's mask. In its place was the oldest piece of Lorcan art they had seen. Hundreds of tiny jewels sparkled on a bronze circle. They formed a whirlpool of colors. With each move of Day Timer's head, the jewels seemed to change into new patterns.

The mask was edged with ruby crystals, like the rays of a red sun. It was a perfect mask for Lorca. It was full of beauty and promise but always changing and somewhat frightening.

"The peddler's wagon is gone," said Day Timer. "Day Timer is gone, too. Now you can meet the one you have been looking for—Almighty Slayer."

CHAPTER 9

Fenton Lewis reached out. "The Wisdom Mask!" he gasped.

The Lorcan knocked his hand away. "I've killed many to guard this mask. I'll not give it to you, to the Ferengi, to Piercing Blade, or to anyone."

"We don't want your mask," said Riker. "But why didn't you tell us who you were?"

"I was tired of fighting battles. I hid the Wisdom Mask and became a peddler. Since then, I have been free. I could stop sharpening my sword long enough to enjoy a sunny day. But now," Almighty Slayer said, "Day Timer has died with his wagon and his pony. Lorca needs a ruler more than a peddler. I was going to the fair to take back my rule. Please come with me. I need friends."

Riker felt strangely tied to Lorca and to the old man in front of him. "All right," he agreed. "We'll stay with you as far as the fair."

Spider Wing was dead. When the ground shook, a huge stone hit and killed him instantly. Piercing

Blade had screamed with anger. But there was no bringing back her friend.

Picard, Worf, and Deanna Troi watched the burial. First, the Lorcans removed Spider Wing's mask. Then they lowered his body into a bog. It disappeared in the wormy mud. When the ceremony was over, Piercing Blade strode toward Jean-Luc.

"Picard," she said, "I want you to wear the Ambassador's Mask. It is trying to find its rightful owner. Perhaps you are the one."

"I am honored," answered Jean-Luc. The captain hoped that he would have better luck than the mask's earlier owners. Two Ferengi had been murdered for it. Now Spider Wing was dead.

"I'll miss him," Piercing Blade whispered, as if reading the captain's thoughts. Then she turned and walked back to her friends.

The peddler's wagon and the pony were gone, but the party continued on toward the fair. The old Lorcan seemed little changed by the Wisdom Mask.

As Riker gathered wood for that night's fire, he watched Almighty Slayer. "The Wisdom Mask chooses who will wear it," the old man had said. Maybe the Wisdom Mask had chosen a warrior, then had waited years for him to become a wise man.

Riker realized that he wanted his friend to win back his throne. This bothered him. The

Prime Directive did not allow such thoughts. For two hundred years, the strong had taken the Wisdom Mask from the weak. Who was he to put an end to this?

A scream split the air. Riker drew his phaser.

"It's Reba!" cried the old Lorcan. He swung the red werjun by its long arms. "She's back!"

Reba chattered. Almighty Slayer nodded. "She says that Piercing Blade's band is not far ahead."

With Reba doing the fishing, there was plenty for dinner. After the meal, Data and Almighty Slayer went into the woods for a talk, but they soon returned. The troop settled around the fire.

Riker was asleep when the noise started. He woke to see the fire casting light on a horrible scene. Fenton Lewis, in his feathered mask, was shooting Almighty Slayer with a phaser. He fired again and again. He tried to tear the Wisdom Mask off the Lorcan's face. But the phaser fire did not hurt the Lorcan, who protected the mask.

Riker could not believe what he was seeing. Fenton Lewis could not believe it either. He turned and ran off into the darkness.

"Lewis stole my phaser," shouted Greenblatt.

Riker ran into the woods. But in the dark he had no chance of catching the ambassador.

When he returned to the fire, Riker was shocked to see Almighty Slayer calmly taking off his mask.

But it was not the face of an old warrior behind the Wisdom Mask. It was the smooth face of an android.

Data quickly handed the Wisdom Mask to the man wearing the Teacher's Mask. The teacher turned around and switched masks, becoming Almighty Slayer. Data took his own mask back.

"You were right," roared the Lorcan. "Lewis was no good. I'm glad *you* decided to be *me!*"

"Data saved my life!" exclaimed Almighty Slayer. "I won't forget that."

"Data should not have risked his life," said Riker. "Day Timer, we will not become part of a power struggle down here."

The old warrior put his arm around Will. "My fine friend, wearer of the Forest Mask, I know just what you will and won't do. I know how loyal you are. If you keep your own people and the Ferengi off my tail, I will be grateful. For now, at least we have gotten rid of a traitor."

Commander Riker looked down the dark road. "I'm going to get Lewis," he promised, "and when I do, I'm going to take him to the farthest starbase I can find. He will never bother Lorca again."

The Thunder Mask and the Ambassador's Mask lay forgotten in the corner of the tent. Jean-Luc kissed Piercing Blade gently.

"Picard?" Piercing Blade whispered when the kiss ended. "When will you leave me?"

"I don't know," he answered honestly. "At the moment, we have no way to go back."

"Then," said Piercing Blade, "we must make the most of the moment." She pulled him close again.

As their lips met, a voice sounded outside. "Halt! Who goes there?"

Piercing Blade jumped. She pulled on her mask. At the same time, Worf's voice roared, "Captain!"

Picard pulled on his own mask. He followed Piercing Blade outside. There, in the light of the campfire, stood a man in a feathered mask.

"Lewis!" exclaimed Picard.

"None other. Please put the swords away. I bring news. I have been with Almighty Slayer."

"Almighty Slayer," gasped Piercing Blade. She drew her sword and pointed it at Fenton Lewis. "If this is a trick, not even the dragon will be able to stop me from taking your head."

Lewis bowed. "No trick, my lady. Almighty Slayer's band is right behind us. I have just come from their camp."

"Did you run away from them, just as you ran away from us?" asked Picard angrily.

"Never mind that," snapped Piercing Blade. "Do you know for sure it's Almighty Slayer? Have you seen the Wisdom Mask? Tell me," she looked closely at him, "what does it look like?"

"Like nothing I've ever seen," said Lewis. "It is a whirlpool of jewels in a circle of rubies."

"That's it!" cried Cold Angel. "My lady, we can have the mask tonight!"

The captain looked at Deanna Troi. He didn't need to see her face to know she sensed violence.

"What other masks did you see in this camp?" Piercing Blade asked Lewis.

"There was one called the Forest Mask."

Piercing Blade nodded. "It can be none other than Almighty Slayer. His first lieutenant always wears the Forest Mask. When I am queen," she promised Lewis, "you shall be rewarded for this." Piercing Blade strode toward her pony.

"She is going to challenge him, isn't she?" Deanna asked Picard. "Can we stop her?"

"No, we must stay out of it," he answered.

"We can't watch them die." Worf murmured.

"Don't you think I want to help them?" asked Picard. "I do, but we can't step in. We have to let things happen as they would without us."

"Can we follow them?" asked Worf.

"Yes," answered the captain. "I want to see that no Ferengi are involved."

Kate Pulaski tried to go to sleep. She watched the sparks of the campfire.

"Are you troubled, Doctor?" asked a voice.

Kate turned to see Data standing nearby. His yellowish eyes glowed in the darkness.

"Would you like to walk?" the android asked.

The two had just strolled into the dark woods when Data held up his hand. "Noises!" he said. "I hear ponies. Perhaps you should turn back."

Kate gripped his arm. "No, Data, I'm with you. We should find out who they are and what they want before we let them see the Wisdom Mask."

Data nodded. "There is nothing in the Prime Directive against asking a few questions."

The teacher and the healer moved forward. Soon they could see lanterns. A tall woman led the pack. Kate stared at her shining star mask.

"Hello," Data called pleasantly. "This is a dark night for traveling."

The star mask leaned forward. "Are you from Almighty Slayer's band? Don't lie to me."

Data was not programmed to lie. "Yes," he said.

"Tell your master to prepare to receive me."

"Who shall we say is calling?" asked Data.

Piercing Blade's voice was cold. "Tell him it's his daughter."

Hidden in the trees, Picard, Worf, and Deanna watched the meeting. They weren't near enough to hear everything. They did hear Piercing Blade say that she was Almighty Slayer's daughter.

Picard blinked in surprise. But the two Lorcans were already heading into the forest. After a few minutes, Piercing Blade's band followed them.

"There is something familiar about that tall Lorcan," said Deanna. "I don't know what it is."

"Let's stay with them," ordered the captain.

Data found Almighty Slayer sleeping behind his mask of swirling colors. The android shook him.

The Lorcan king rolled onto his back. His old eyes blinked at Data. "What is it, my friend?"

"Your daughter is here."

"What?" he roared, wide awake. His voice brought the others to their feet.

Dr. Pulaski pointed down the road. Lights already shone between the tree trunks. "We're going to have visitors very soon. They know that Almighty Slayer is here with the Wisdom Mask."

"Lewis must have told them," Riker said. "How else could they know?"

Almighty Slayer stomped around the fire. *"I have no daughter!"* he shouted. Then he stabbed the air with his sword. "We can beat them!"

"I told you this before, Day Timer," said Riker. "We are not going to mix in your affairs."

"My affairs? My affairs will be spilled out all over this ground if you don't help me. I'm no match for Piercing Blade in a duel. Not anymore."

"Then you do know this woman?" asked Pulaski. "She says she is your daughter."

"Daughter or not, she has only one thing on her mind—to take my mask."

"Day Timer, what would you do if you didn't have us?" asked Riker.

The king's shoulders drooped. "I probably would have stayed a peddler." Everyone was silent. Suddenly the *Enterprise*, the Federation, even the stars seemed far away.

"Phasers on stun," Riker muttered. "Keep them hidden. Maybe we can talk our way out of this."

"Hail, Almighty Slayer," called a voice. "Prepare to receive Lady Piercing Blade."

The small party appeared. Two pages held their lanterns high. Almighty Slayer walked toward them. He stood with his hands on his hips.

Piercing Blade shook her shining mask. "So, Father, you have come back to the land of the living?"

"You may call me a worm in the mud if you like, but you can't call me your father."

"Right." She nodded. "Women are playthings to

you. Like my mother. You never treated her with respect to the day she died."

Almighty Slayer lowered his head. "I am not that man anymore," he whispered.

But Piercing Blade wasn't listening. She drew her sword. "You have had the Wisdom Mask for thirty cycles. Now it is time to give it up." She pointed her sword at the old warrior. "Almighty Slayer, by the fire of the dragon, I challenge your right to wear the Wisdom Mask." Her green eyes flashed. "Hand it over or die at your daughter's hand."

Data moved to Riker. "That is not their whole company. I count four hiding in the forest."

"I hate this," said Riker. "We can't help him. The Wisdom Mask is his. He must defend it."

But Almighty Slayer had other ideas. He turned to Data. "My friend, will you fight for me as you did last night?"

Data stepped forward. "I am your friend, Almighty Slayer. But you have not ruled as king for a long time. You should think about passing the rule to someone who is younger and more willing to serve."

"This is very strange," said Worf. He was hiding behind a tree with Picard and Troi. "It seems his own people are not going to back him."

Picard pointed to Almighty Slayer's followers. "There is something odd about them."

Almighty Slayer drew his sword. "I shall protect the Wisdom Mask with my life. After today I shall have no child."

"Or I shall have no father," said Piercing Blade. She stepped down from her pony.

Their swords clashed. Piercing Blade was stronger. She pushed her father to his knees. But the old warrior grabbed her foot and tripped her. He slashed up with his sword, slicing her shoulder.

Jean-Luc moved forward. But he felt a hand on his arm. He turned to see Deanna, shaking her head.

"Captain," she said, "it is not our fight."

Blood was flowing from her wound, but Piercing Blade fought on. "Give me the mask, you old werjun," shouted Piercing Blade.

Piercing Blade swung her sword, knocking the king off his feet. When he tried to get up, he found Piercing Blade's sword at his throat.

Before Piercing Blade could use her sword, Data raced across the road. He grabbed her arm.

"Data!" shouted Riker. "Don't hurt her!"

Cold Angel rode forward, his sword drawn. But he was stopped by a cry from Deanna Troi.

"Stop! These are our friends! Will Riker, is that you?"

"Yes!" exclaimed Riker. He tore off his mask. Deanna ran toward him, throwing off her own.

Dr. Pulaski tore off her mask. So did Data and Ensign Greenblatt. From the trees, Worf and Picard ran into the light, ripping off their own masks.

The Lorcans hid their eyes from the sight of all the naked faces. But the laughter and cries of joy made them peek. They saw one of the happiest meetings ever to take place in the galaxy.

Lieutenant Commander Data let go of Piercing Blade's arm. "I am sorry. You may have the Wisdom Mask, but you may not slay Almighty Slayer."

"I never wanted to kill him," she breathed. "All of you are from the ship in the sky?"

"Yes," the android nodded. He did not notice the man in the feathered Messenger's Mask sneaking up on Almighty Slayer.

The messenger snatched the Wisdom Mask off the old man. Ensign Greenblatt was the closest. She grabbed for the mask. But Fenton Lewis had set his stolen phaser to kill. He hit her with a red beam. Greenblatt fell to the ground, dead. Lewis ran into the trees.

Shock turned to anger in the early Lorcan dawn. With their own phasers drawn, Worf, Riker, and Picard went after the killer. The three officers moved carefully into the forest.

At least we are together again, Riker thought, even if our ordeal is not over yet.

CHAPTER 10

Dr. Pulaski was on her knees beside the body of the young ensign. She looked up at Data and Deanna Troi and shook her head. "Pulaski to the *Enterprise*," she said into her communicator.

"*Enterprise* here," answered Geordi.

"I have news for you," Kate began. "First, let me tell you we have found Captain Picard, Counselor Troi, and Lieutenant Worf. They are all fine."

Kate could hear the cheers on the *Enterprise* bridge. She hated to give the bad news. "We have a body to beam up. It is Ensign Greenblatt. She's dead, Geordi. Lock on to my signal."

Piercing Blade bent down and picked up the Ambassador's Mask that Picard had thrown aside. "Cover yourself, father. You deserve this mask more than those naked-faced off-worlders. Now *they* have our Wisdom Mask."

"Fenton Lewis is our enemy as much as yours," said Kate. "He killed one of our own people!"

"From now on," said Deanna Troi, "we won't wear masks. You will see us as we really are."

Almighty Slayer pulled the Ambassador's Mask over his face. "I have spent many days with these people," he said. "I don't believe that they want the Wisdom Mask for themselves. They didn't trust the messenger, this Fenton Lewis. In fact, he tried to steal the mask earlier, and Data protected me."

"I let the messenger bring us here," cried Piercing Blade. "Picard warned me about him, but I was too eager to face you, Father."

Almighty Slayer went to his daughter's side. He put his arm around her. "I always knew I'd have to face you, and that you would best me."

"But now neither of us has the Wisdom Mask," said Piercing Blade angrily.

"We brought Fenton Lewis here," said Kate Pulaski. She began to tend to the Lorcans' wounds. "I'm sure Captain Picard, Commander Riker, and Lieutenant Worf are doing all they can to bring back the Wisdom Mask."

"They had better be," snarled Cold Angel. "Because you are our prisoners until it's back."

Fenton Lewis crashed through the woods like a hunted animal. He wanted to get as far as he could from the others. So far, he hadn't fired his phaser at them, but he would do so if they got too close.

He held his stolen prize tight. He was now the owner of Lorca's Wisdom Mask. He was the king.

But he still had work to do. He had to hire an army of soldiers from around the galaxy to help him hold his throne. He patted the phaser. Until then, this weapon would do. The Lorcans could not stand up to a phaser. If they accepted him as king, the Ferengi and everyone else would do the same. He had the Wisdom Mask. They had to accept him.

But all that would come later. Now, he needed to hide until the *Enterprise* gave up and moved on.

He saw a light far ahead of him. If it was a party of Lorcans, the Wisdom Mask might persuade them to help him. If it didn't, the phaser would.

Jean-Luc Picard saw the light, too. "There's something ahead of us," he told Worf and Riker.

"Lewis will head for it," Riker said.

"Why do you think that, Number One?"

"Because he has the Wisdom Mask. He will want to be a big shot and try it out."

"I agree," said Worf, "and with the phaser, he won't be worried about anything."

"Very well," said the captain. "Let's move toward the light—carefully."

"I have heard that the Wisdom Mask chooses its owner," said Data. He was watching Kate care for the wounds of the father and daughter. "That means that if Piercing Blade is meant to wear it, it will come back to her."

"The Wisdom Mask goes to the strongest!" said Cold Angel. "The one with the quickest sword."

"True," said Almighty Slayer. "That is how I held on to it. But do you know how I came by the Wisdom Mask?"

"I've heard this story before," sighed Piercing Blade.

"You can never hear it enough," Almighty Slayer replied. He stood up tall. "I was only a page, but I was young and strong. I had no thoughts of the Wisdom Mask. I was part of Whistling Arrow's band. We were chasing the old king, just as you have been chasing me. But Burning Cloud was a clever old king. By the time we caught up with him, he was naked-faced. He had buried the mask.

"Burning Cloud died at our hands, rather than tell us where he'd hidden the mask. We looked for weeks, digging up every stone and mound of clay."

Almighty Slayer pointed to the clouds. "It was on a morning darker than this. The others were asleep. I saw a werjun up in a tree. He was not the least bit afraid of me. He swung to another tree—chattering. I followed him. He moved slowly, as if he *wanted* me to follow.

"He led me to an old stump. He reached into a hole in the stump and tried to pull something out. I went to help. Imagine my surprise when I saw red rubies shining within that deep hole. I had the Wisdom Mask. It had been given to me by a werjun! I knew then that *I* was meant to rule Lorca.

"I threw the Page's Mask aside. I put on the Wisdom Mask. I had to kill many warriors, including Whistling Arrow, to keep it. But I held on to that mask for thirty winters and thirty summers until today. I have remained friends with the werjuns. So you see, Piercing Blade, the Wisdom Mask will be yours, if you are worthy of it."

The old warrior sat back down on the ground. "Now," he said, "I am tired. I've earned my rest."

"We shall wait," declared Piercing Blade. "But only until the sun has risen above the treetops."

Picard, Riker, and Worf crawled forward. A few rays of sun came through the trees now. They could see red-masked guards stopping Fenton Lewis as he strolled into their camp.

Jean-Luc stopped close enough to hear voices and to see the camp clearly. The light they had seen was a big globe. It floated above three huts. The guards led Fenton Lewis into the center of the camp. The globe turned bright orange. Seconds later, two silver-masked Ferengi came out of a hut.

"What have we here?" asked a Ferengi. "A Lorcan with a Federation phaser?"

"Everybody stay in front of me," Lewis ordered. He waved the phaser.

One of the red-masked raiders dropped to his knees. "The Wisdom Mask," he cried.

"Who are you?" asked a Ferengi.

"What you call me doesn't matter," answered Lewis. "What matters is that I am the ruler of Lorca. I have the mask."

"But you are only one person," a Ferengi pointed out. "You are alone."

"One person with one phaser," said Lewis. "I will be happy to do business with you. But I will also be happy to do business without you. Wouldn't it be wise to have someone you can deal with as ruler of Lorca? I'll make it worth your while."

"Well," said one Ferengi. "We can start the trading with the Wisdom Mask. How much?"

Lewis shook his head. "This mask is not for sale. But if you'll help me now, I'll repay you later—in masks or in anything you want."

"But that mask is here now. All those other masks aren't. Why don't you give it to us?"

Lewis waved the phaser at them. "I'm done talking. The Wisdom Mask is mine. Now stand over there, so I can get through your camp."

But neither of the Ferengi moved. "I'm afraid we can't let you leave."

The second Ferengi drew a whip from his belt.

Lewis fired his phaser at the Ferengi with the whip. The beam bent off into the trees.

Lewis fired again and again. Each time the phaser beam bounced off an invisible force field.

"Antiphaser field," explained a Ferengi. He pointed to the orange ball over their heads. "It blocks Federation weapons."

Fenton turned to run. But three raiders grabbed him They dragged him by his long hair to face the Ferengi. "Let's see who you really are," laughed a Ferengi. He pulled off the Wisdom Mask.

"I am a Federation ambassador!" gasped Fenton Lewis. "I demand fair treatment."

"I think we are in luck," said a Ferengi. He looked at the globe. "Check this human's identity."

A purple beam shot out of the globe. It surrounded Lewis. He cried out in pain. When the light faded, he moaned and coughed.

A high voice came from the globe. "Federation Ambassador Fenton Lewis. Murdered two Ferengi. Sentence: death."

The Ferengi nodded to each other.

Riker knew what was coming. He raised up in his hiding place. But Jean-Luc put out his hand.

"Our phasers are useless in there," Picard whispered.

Riker bit his lip as a red beam shot from the globe. It circled Lewis's body. He twitched and screamed, but only for a minute. Then he lay still.

The Ferengi again addressed the glowing ball. "We have a body to beam up: one human criminal named Fenton Lewis."

The other Ferengi held the Wisdom Mask close. "Double the guard," he ordered the raiders. "There are probably more of them out there."

Picard touched Worf's and Riker's arms. They turned and moved back the way they had come. They crawled to a point where they could no longer see the light of the Ferengi camp.

"That ends the Fenton Lewis problem," said Riker.

"But not the missing mask problem," said Jean-Luc. "There has to be a way to get it back."

Commander Riker stroked his beard. "I know how we can get in there. Except for mine and Day Timer's, all the masks we wore were old Raider's Masks. They had been taken in battle and painted over. All we have to do is paint them red again. We can walk right into their camp."

"An excellent idea," said Worf. "I volunteer."

Jean-Luc smiled. "It's a good idea, but too dangerous. You wouldn't stand a chance, not unless you had a Lorcan with you to say and do the right thing."

"I know that place," said Cold Angel. "It's an old gathering spot for raiders."

The Lorcans and sky people stood in a circle. There were six bare faces and six masked ones.

Riker laid out the Teacher's Mask, the Archer's Mask, and the Healer's Mask. "Those masks belonged to raiders before," he explained. "We can paint them red and join the raiders' band. Then we'll wait for a chance to steal the Wisdom Mask."

"It would work!" agreed Cold Angel.

"Your plan has a chance, Number One," Picard said. "But remember, our phasers will be useless. You would need swords to fight your way out."

"I agree," said Piercing Blade. "That is why Cold Angel, Medicine Maker, and I will be there."

But Medicine Maker stepped forward. "Pardon me, my lady. You cannot pass yourself off as a raider. There are some things that no mask can hide. Besides," he added, "Lorca needs a living ruler, not another dead hero."

"Riker, Cold Angel, and I are the ones to do it,"

said Almighty Slayer. "Cold Angel and I have the best chance of fooling the other raiders. Riker seems to know something about these Ferengi."

"That is a logical choice," said Data. "As soon as they have the mask, Commander Riker can signal the *Enterprise* to beam them up."

"Very well," said the captain. "Number One, do just as Data suggested."

"I've got to make red paint," said Slayer. "Piercing Blade, can your pages help me?"

"Certainly, Father," she replied. Then she turned to the captain. Her eyes were sad. "What will you be doing, Jean-Luc Picard?" she asked.

"I must return to my ship. My crew has been like Lorca, a people without a leader."

Piercing Blade sighed. She moved closer to him. But Data broke in. "I need to contact the ship, sir. Shall I tell Geordi you're beaming up?"

"Yes. Five to beam up—Dr. Pulaski, Counselor Troi, Lieutenant Worf, Data, and I." Then Jean-Luc's eyes went again to Piercing Blade. He wanted to remember everything about her.

"Come back some day, Picard," she said.

He squeezed her hand. "Rule wisely."

"Captain," said Data, "they are ready."

"Good-bye," whispered Picard. He pulled away from Piercing Blade. He was joined by Dr. Pulaski, Counselor Troi, Lieutenant Worf, and Data.

"I'll miss this place," said Deanna.

"Yes," Kate Pulaski said. "But it'll be nice to sleep in a bed again."

Jean-Luc stared at Piercing Blade as he disappeared.

Almighty Slayer reached out to the place they had stood. Then he asked, "Data, are you sure that doesn't hurt?"

Data answered, "I do not know for certain, but some people says it tickles."

"Come on," said Cold Angel. He stepped off the road into the dark forest. Their swords at their sides, Riker and Slayer followed him.

The woods were thick, and Almighty Slayer soon seemed tired. The group walked on in silence. Finally a light shone in the forest ahead of them. Even though it was cold, Will found his hands were sweating. His phaser was going to be of no use, and the sword at his side felt strange.

"Let us do the talking," Slayer warned.

As they drew closer, Riker held up his hand. "Wait," he whispered. Something was different. Before the globe had floated above the camp. Now it seemed to shine weakly from the ground.

Then the wind shifted. The smell of death blew through the forest. The Lorcans drew their swords.

Riker reached for his communicator. Then they saw the Ferengi raiders laying dead on the ground. The Ferengi globe throbbed weakly in the clay. A Lorcan sword was stuck in the middle of the broken orb. Beside the globe lay a dead raider wearing the Wisdom Mask.

"I think they're all dead," said Cold Angel. "It looks as if they jumped the Ferengi and then fought among themselves."

Almighty Slayer nodded. "They kept challenging each other until there were none left. The winner had just enough strength to put on the mask before he died."

Cold Angel carefully took the Wisdom Mask off the dead raider.

"What will you do now?" Riker asked.

"My daughter will wear the Wisdom Mask," answered Almighty Slayer. "She might have to bash one or two heads to hold on to it, but that will be the easy part. I shall wear the Ambassador's Mask. I shall try to deal with you off-worlders."

"Let's go," said Cold Angel. With the Wisdom Mask under his arm, he marched into the woods.

Will clasped Almighty Slayer's arm. "Good luck to you. We'll try to return soon."

"Come to the fair," said the old warrior proudly. "See my daughter crowned queen."

Riker watched the Lorcans disappear into the woods. Then he tapped his communicator.

"Back so soon, Number One?" Captain Picard said cheerily as Riker entered the Bridge. "The Ferengi must not have put up much of a fight."

"They couldn't," Will answered. He explained the scene at the Ferengi camp.

"I have news, too," said the captain. "Starfleet is letting us stay here a few more days. They want to set up relations with Lorca. I thought you and Data could go to the fair. You could talk to Piercing Blade about joining the Federation."

"Sir? Wouldn't you rather do that yourself?"

Jean-Luc shook his head and smiled sadly. "No. I would rather not say good-bye to her again."

Riker and Data stepped onto the transporter platform. There were no phasers and no masks on this trip. They were coming in peace, and they were coming as themselves.

The commander and the android beamed right into the middle of the Lorcan fair. Luckily, they were well hidden behind a stage. They peeked out into the crowd. Immediately, they saw a familiar figure in a familiar mask. When the Lorcan came close, out they popped.

"My friends! It's about time you returned!" cried the happy voice behind the Ambassador's Mask. "Riker, Data, what a welcome sight!"

Almighty Slayer clasped their arms. "Come with me," he said excitedly. "I have something for you."

He led his friends to a tent. He ducked inside and came out with two sparkling new masks. They were painted a pale orange shot with red streaks over the eyes. The masks clearly suggested the Lorcan sky. Black jewels circled the mouth.

"We call it the Federation Mask," said Almighty Slayer proudly.

"Thank you," said Riker. "We will keep them aboard our ship forever in the hope of returning."

"Let's go see the queen!" said the ex-king.

A line waited outside Piercing Blade's tent. The Lorcans had come to wish their new queen well.

Inside the tent, it was dark and cool. There were no swords or weapons in sight. Piercing Blade was dressed in a simple purple gown. Lamplight shone on the swirling jewels of the Wisdom Mask. The queen saw her new visitors. "My father knew you would come back," she said. She took Riker's hand. "He has proved to be very wise."

"Your fair is wonderful," said Riker. "We are

happy to see you have set up your leadership so peacefully.

The queen nodded. Then she looked past him. "There are just the two of you? Jean-Luc Picard didn't come?" Before Riker could answer, she continued. "He will come soon. We are going to make Lorca safe enough for all to visit. We have asked all Lorcans to lay down their weapons. We will trade no more with the Ferengi. We want to accept the sky people as our people. The dragon once took you away from us, but now you have returned."

Will smiled behind his new mask. He touched his communicator. "Riker to the bridge."

"Picard here," answered the captain.

Piercing Blade leaned forward at the sound of the voice.

"Captain, you would not believe how wonderful and peaceful it is down here," Riker said. "I am with the queen and her father. They assure us the planet is safe for visitors. They have even made us a special mask. I suggest we stay a few more days and give everyone shore leave. Yourself included."

"This is good to hear," answered the captain. "Give the queen and her father my regards. Tell them there are many who are eager to visit Lorca."

Maybe Will Riker imagined it, but he thought he saw the Wisdom Mask smile.